Social Media: How to Skyrocket Your Business Through Social Media Marketing!

Master Facebook, Twitter, YouTube, Instagram, & LinkedIn

D1306101

Table of Contents

INTRODUCTION:

Marketing these days is totally different compared to what it was just a generation ago. If you're like me who has been around, you'll definitely agree with that statement. The specificity, the reach and the quality of marketing activities today is something that would've been considered a figment of someone's crazy imagination a mere 15 years ago.

The single biggest difference? The Internet, which has totally revamped the world as well as how it does business these days. As New York Times bestselling author Thomas Friedman would call it, the world has become flat. The emergence and popularity of the Internet have led to a myriad of social media platforms. These enable us to communicate and connect with the people around us in many different ways at the click of a button, even those people residing on the opposite side of the world. We can share things, like things, share that we like things, with someone ten thousand miles away, in less than a minute. The world we live in now is startlingly different than the one we lived in only a few short decades ago.

What separates modern day marketing and conventional or traditional marketing activities is the Internet. In particular, the popularity of social media has become the single biggest defining factor. Couple that with the advent and proliferation of portable devices such as laptops, tablets and smartphones and the social media wildfire can only be expected to continue growing and spreading at a very rapid pace as is happening now. In fact, it's fast approaching a situation where it may be virtually impossible to hear of people who don't have Facebook accounts.

Take my mother, for example, who is already 68 years old and has her own active Facebook and email accounts. On the other, less serious hand, consider my niece who is just a few months old but already has her own Facebook account. Well, that's courtesy of her mother of course but the point being is that's how wide and far reaching the Internet is, particularly social media. As such, it sure makes it a very formidable marketing force.

There are people, particularly business owners, who fear that social media is a temporary star, a modern day fad. They might hesitate to invest time, money, and other resources into something they fear will quickly fade, but we are here to disillusion these individuals of any such concerns and misgivings by illustrating the myriad of benefits that utilizing social media marketing will bring you.

In this book, we'll discuss what's probably the single most important aspect of modern day marketing, which is social media. We'll also look at the different ways that you can leverage the different social media platforms to get your business out there to anyone in the world. So from your mind to practically anywhere in the world, may your business be promoted far and wide!

CHAPTER 1

MARKETING 101

As defined in the website business www.dictionary.com, marketing is an activity or process conducted by management in which services and goods are transferred from the concept stage to the hands of the customers. This process includes managing 4 crucial elements of marketing, also known as the 4 Ps. These are product, price, place and promotion. So before we go to the nitty-gritty of social media marketing, let's first take a quick look at these 4 important elements of marketing to better understand social media marketing principles later on.

PRODUCT

In marketing terms, product refers to identifying, selecting and developing a service or a good that will be sold to customers. To come up with very good products that will sell, business owners and managers must learn to see their business' products from the point of view of an outsider, which takes into consideration their planned or current products' ability to meet their target market's needs and wants as well as the available competing products in the market. To do this successfully business owners and managers would do well to be skilled in putting themselves in someone else's shoes in order to make an informed and objective choice on what product they might be able to sell well. They also must be able to scope out and analyze their competition- a duplicate, or superior product being sold by a competitor for a similar or better price is a surefire way to ensure your own product's failure. Since anyone marketing their product needs to optimize their potential sales, ensuring you offer products with better quality, prices, or convenience can be vital in ensuring that you overtake your competition, instead of the other way around.

PRICE

When talking of price, we refer to the value at which you'll sell your services or goods. Of all the important features of your services and products, price is probably the most competitive one. What this means is many businesses often compete for customers by trying to lower prices.

When it comes to business, there are situations where prices must be lowered in order to remain competitive and survive. There are situations too, when raising prices is perfectly acceptable, even recommended. If your business happens to be in a very competitive industry, you're most likely marketing strategy is keeping prices low. If your business is in an industry with very little or virtually no competition, you may enjoy the luxury of increasing your goods or services' prices.

Keep in mind the price of your products or services isn't just about the monetary value but also takes into consideration the overall value, which includes flexible and easy payment terms and free items, among others. Special promotions, be it rebates, coupons, or other temporary sales, can help to ensure your customers that they are getting the best value for their money. Everyone loves a discount, so marking something down to a lower price, provided you ensure you charge enough to make a healthy profit, can really get your clients excited about making their purchase and raise the odds that they'll recommend buying from you to their friends and family, thus gaining you further customers.

PLACE

Place means selecting a distribution channel for making sure that your services or products reach your customers' place or where they're actually sold. As a business owner, you should regularly evaluate your sales people and customers meeting points.

There are situations where you need to change the location of your business in order to experience significant growth in sales. The primary consideration in terms of choosing a place from which to distribute your services or goods is your customers' convenience. It doesn't matter if your product or service is the cheapest on earth if the customer has to go through so much inconvenience to buy or avail of them. Think of it this way, would you buy a brand, spanking new iPhone 6S for only $100 if the store is located in Iraq or Syria? I don't think so. Of course, selling from a prime location usually comes with higher costs for you, but people will pay quite the premium to avoid a time-consuming or unpleasant trip. We all are familiar with the old sayings 'That's the price of convenience' and 'Time is money', and when it comes to place, these sayings will be proven true time and again. It is usually well worth the greater initial investment for the benefit of getting away with increasing your prices over the less convenient shops. Additionally, if you are located in an ideal location, you will be visible to more potential clients, thus raising awareness of your business without needing to spend so much on advertising to do so. As we move ever more into the digital age, physical location is no longer as essential as it once was. There is so much we can accomplish online, enabling us to cater to even people on the other side of the planet. Additionally, with the advent of handheld technology, including advanced phones, touch pads, and tablets, people can access information and shops stored online no matter where they roam or what they are doing.

PROMOTION

When we talk about promotion, we refer to the activity of formulating strategies and implementing them in order to make people aware of your products or services. Promotion basically includes all the different ways you can tell your current and prospective buyers about your services or products. And an important part of promotion is positioning, which is the art of placing your service or product on top – or near the top – of your target and current markets' minds.

Promotional changes – regardless of the size and scope – can significantly affect the level of your sales. An example of this is how experienced ad copywriters can significantly influence or affect a product or service's sales simply by changing one or two words in the headline of their advertisements. As a business owner, you should regularly experiment in terms of various approaches in promoting your services and products. And keep in mind that while many approaches can work for your business, all of them don't work forever. If you experiment on a regular basis, you can enjoy the benefit of having several promotional alternatives ready on hand to replace your current promotional approach the moment it becomes stale. By ensuring your products and business seem fresh and adaptable, you put yourself ahead of your competitors. Even small changes, if well applied, can cause prospective customers to notice your business while overlooking the businesses of those around you, leading you to become the dominant supplier in your area with just a bit of clever marketing.

In this book, we'll focus on this last P, promoting your products or services by getting them to your target markets on virtually every smartphone, tablet and computer in the world that's connected to the Internet. With the ubiquity of the Internet these days, this allows your business to reach out to customers in a way previous generations could never have imagined. A whole new world of possibilities exists with this software, and with a bit of work and imagination, it can be harnessed to create profit and success for your budding business.

CHAPTER 2

SOCIAL MEDIA 101

As an activity or process, social media may be defined as an interaction tool used by people for exchanging, sharing or creating information and ideas in virtual or digital communities over the Internet. From an invention point of view, we can look at social media as web-based applications that provide us with opportunities for interacting and connecting with many people. It is also a platform by which communities and individuals are able to modify, discuss, co-create and share content that are generated or created by other users. Immediacy, usability permanence, reach, frequency and quality are just some of the qualities that make social media significantly different from – and superior to –industrial or traditional media. You may already be familiar with the most popular social media websites like Instagram, Twitter, and Facebook, and there are many others out there that also enjoy great or growing numbers of followers and fans just waiting for you to utilize.

When you look at it, the number of people on social media websites can be quite staggering and as such, they're considered to be any marketing professional's heaven. To give you an idea just how staggering, it's estimated, for example, that Facebook has more than 1.3 billion active users, about half of which log on to their accounts on a daily basis. It is also estimated that Twitter has more than 615 million active users, and this is only a glimmer of the billions of active social media accounts your customers are using all around the world. With such kinds of numbers, marketing professionals can swim in an ocean of prospects.

Another important difference between social media and traditional or industrial marketing is the engagement of customers. By engaging customers, social media marketing provides customers the opportunity to participate or take ownership of a particular brand, message, service or product by liking them, commenting on what's happening to them or asking questions about them. Because customers and potential customers get a sense of ownership or partnership in a brand, message, service or product, the possibility or likelihood of increased sales is significantly higher. This can be easily accomplished by communicating with your clientele, and is further promoted by polls or other promotions that allow your customers the opportunity to really feel involved and valued by your business.

THE ROLE OF SOCIAL MEDIA IN MODERN DAY BUSINESS MANAGEMENT

Back in the day, any interested customer or prospect can only get information on a product, service or the company providing them by contacting the company directly or through their representatives. Industrial or traditional marketing focused its resources on trade shows, mass advertising, print media and PR to create and build awareness of services and products. It used to be too, that the primary way for business owners and customers to interact was through cold calls and direct mail only, where any potential customers or fresh leads were just passed on or transferred to a company or business' sales team for following up. Naturally, this resulted in inefficient, indirect communication, which rarely benefits either companies or customers.

But Google changed all that. Because of Google, companies began to look for new ways of generating sales leads, particularly through the use of email marketing, pay-per-click (PPC) advertising and search engine optimization (SEO), all of which served to funnel sales prospects to their respective websites. While email marketing is today's version of what used to be called the direct mail marketing, pay-per-click, also referred to as cost-per-click, is a way of advertising that seeks to funnel prospective clients to their businesses' websites by paying websites owners whenever people click on ads that appear on their websites. Search engine optimization refers to the process or activity of managing a particular website's content in such a way that it places highly in search results for particular keywords or topics in different search engine websites, particularly Google, Yahoo! and Bing. There are code words and strategies that companies can master in order to ensure their website will be amongst the top results for the exact customer base they are trying to target, ensuring the greatest likelihood of those who come across their website actually making a purchase. These strategies enable businesses to, by utilizing the technological wonder of the Internet, target customers on a more personal, individual level, lessening the need for mass advertising and instead honing in primarily on the people most inclined to appreciate your specific product.

With the advent of the Internet, businesses have also learned to generate content such as white papers - also known as authoritative reports on particular topics of interest for certain target markets - and webinars, which are live or recorded seminars that are shown over the Internet. These two help businesses convert visits to their websites to sales leads.

But the efficiency of the Internet also brought with it some very interesting challenges. One of which is sending sales leads to salespeople prematurely and such relatively quick send-offs led to wastage of sales leads. As a result, businesses learned first to nurture their leads and were forced to create programs that were able to better qualify hot sales leads from those with low or no potential – at least not yet. Doing so allowed businesses to refer to their sales teams only those sales prospects that have high potential. And by identifying those leads that don't have much potential yet, they can first nurture them through regular communications until such time that they become qualified hot leads. This enables businesses to avoid wasting their sales team's potential on currently unfulfilling clientele, but to gently groom such clientele for future advertising campaigns, leading to eventual sales.

And it's in this nurturing process where social media comes in. It does so by engaging potential customers with regular communications that are designed to convert them into hot leads or leads with good sales potential. In particular, up-and-coming and small businesses benefit greatly from using social media because unlike big corporations, they normally don't have big budgets for marketing and advertisement. This is why social media can be a great starting point for attracting customers and growing your business. The ease of the process and the low cost make it an affordable investment that can enable you to expand your business more than our predecessors would have believed possible.

WHY USE SOCIAL MEDIA MARKETING?

For many modern-day entrepreneurs, the big marketing thing these days is social media. For some, it's just a temporary but the very powerful business fad or trend that every entrepreneur and marketing professional must take advantage of while still hot. But to others, it's just a popular word that offers no practical advantage and can be a very complicated and steep learning curve.

Social media has somehow earned a reputation with some people as simply being a passing marketing fad or trend and as such, one that's unprofitable – simply because it appeared rather quickly. Few companies are inspired to work through learning a new and sometimes challenging system when the older methods seem tried and true, especially if they do not expect such a method to be sustainable. They view it as a flash-in-the-pan so to speak. But statistics tend to offer a different take on it, a very different one.

Popular inbound marketing software platform Hubspot noted that in 2014, 92% of marketing professionals said that social media marketing played an important role in their businesses with as much as 80% of them claiming that their websites' traffic went up because of it. Social Media Examiner – a United States-based media company, said that 97% of marketing professionals use social media marketing, although 85% of those they surveyed admitted not knowing which social media tools are the best ones to use.

Clearly, this shows that social media marketing has great potential for jacking up sales but on the other hand, the ability to use it optimally for achieving such results is still lacking in general. If you're generally clueless as to how you can use social media marketing to your business' advantage, here's a list of that can help you become familiar with the benefits your business may enjoy from using this kind of marketing activity.

BETTER BRAND AWARENESS

Consider every chance you get how to increase your business's visibility and the syndicated content is very valuable. And one of the best new ways to showcase your business's content invoice is through your social media networks. Using them can make your business more accessible and easier to contact, making it more recognizable and familiar to your current, as well as prospective customers.

A good example of this is a regular user of Twitter, who finds out about your business and its products or services only after he or she stumbled upon it in his or her Twitter news feed. Another good example would be an otherwise apathetic potential customer who may become more familiar with your product or service only after he or she sees it on multiple social networks. In these ways, social media can allow you to attract a far more widespread customer base as it enables you to get your business out there on the social feeds of your potential clientele- even the ones that would have been challenging to target without this technology. By seeing your brand appearing as they browse through Twitter or by noticing that some of their friends liked you on Facebook, you are attracting more and more people to your business, ultimately resulting in more sales for your business.

HIGHER CUSTOMER LOYALTY

A published report by Texas Tech University noted that businesses that use social media to engage customers to enjoy more loyalty from them compared to those who don't. The report's conclusion is that businesses must make full use of available social media tools to connect with their audience. An open and strategic social media plan can be greatly beneficial in terms of improving customers' brand loyalty.

In another study, this time by Convince&Convert, reported that about 53% of Americans who are followers of particular brands in social media tend to be more loyal to such brands compared to those who don't.

The result of these studies likely is linked to the fact that social media can target customers on a more personal level than all previous forms of advertising. It enables you to solicit public opinion via polls, games, and other fun and engaging activities that attract customers to your business, and then maintain their attention. This is accomplished by the fact that social media allows your clients to feel like they have a role in shaping your business, your products, your methods- they feel valued and important to the processes your business goes through, and as such they become loyal to the businesses that enable them to experience such positive feelings.

MORE CONVERSION OPPORTUNITIES

Whenever you post something on your business' social media pages, you provide an opportunity for your business to convince its audience to perform a particular action, which is called "conversion." When you build your business' following, you immediately gain access to all types of customers - old ones, recent ones and new ones. Further, you get the opportunity to engage or interact with them.

Every comment, video, blog post, or image that you share on your business' social media pages gives people the opportunity to react, and these reactions can potentially lead them to visit your site – potential conversions. Just keep in mind that not all interactions with your business lead to conversions but that each and every positive interaction raises the chances of an actual conversion. Any positive reaction is likely to raise awareness, and the more awareness raised, the greater the likelihood of gaining conversions. Social media marketing is accomplished, in part, via word of mouth. The more quality posts and content you share, the more your friends and followers like, favorite, or share it, and the more awareness and interest in your company spreads.

If your business' website suffers from low click-through rates, the huge amount of opportunities available on social media can prove to be especially helpful. And if you'd like to have any chance of conversion, the first and most important things you need are opportunities for such.

HIGHER RATES FOR CONVERSION

In several distinct ways, social media marketing can lead to higher rate of conversion for your business' websites. Possibly the most significant way it does so is through a "humanization effect", i.e., it makes your business more like a person instead of a, well, business. Social media gives businesses opportunities to act and behave as if they're people, which is important because the truth people naturally prefer doing business with people and not just with lifeless institutions. It has also been shown in studies that social media has a much, much higher lead-to-close rate, which is the percentage of sales leads that eventually buy a company's products or services, compared to outbound marketing. Customers are more inclined to trust a business that comes off a personable and likable- like someone they could be friends with, instead of simply a cold, detached institution. Getting to engage with your business in a way that feels intimate to your clientele can gain their trust and loyalty, and the communication methods social media offers can enable you to accomplish exactly that.

Having a lot of social media followers can also improve your business' trust and credibility with customers – a form of social proof. Most people are, to some extent, followers. If their friends or those they follow are a part of your customer base, new customers are far more inclined to deem your business likely to be a good one worthy of their support. Because of this, it makes a lot of sense to use social media to make significant improvements in your business websites' current conversion rates.

STRONGER BRAND AUTHORITY

When you regularly interact with your customers, you show good faith to other prospective customers. When customers want to brag about or complement your service or product, they'll most probably turn to the Internet and in particular, social media. And when they post about your service or product, the chances are that new audiences or potential customers may want to follow your product or service brand on social media for more updates. Your product or service will start to become more valuable and authoritative once more people talk about it over social media. Also, your product or service's reach and visible authority can significantly improve if you also interact with some of the major players in your industry on Facebook, Twitter or other popular social media sites. Friendly banter, with both your customers and your competitors, grants you an increasingly well-developed social face for your business, enabling you to project a social image that your customers and potential customers will come to trust and appreciate.

HIGHER INBOUND WEBSITE TRAFFIC

If you don't use social media, the inbound traffic for your product's or service's website can be significantly limited to just the individuals who are looking for keywords where your site currently ranks for or people who may already be familiar with your product or service. Each and every profile you create on social media can be a potential path that leads people to your business's website and each and every content you post or syndicate on them can provide new opportunities for fresh, new site visitors. The more social media sites you take the time to utilize effectively, the more conversions you can expect to gain. If the quality of the content you post on your social media pages is good, you can reasonably expect your websites' inbound traffic to increase, which can give you more leads and conversions.

LOWER COST OF MARKETING YOUR PRODUCTS AND SERVICES

It is estimated that around 84% of Internet marketers believe that only up to 6 hours of effort every week is more than enough to generate higher inbound traffic for their websites. Actually, 6 hours may not even be considered a significant investment for a very big marketing channel like social media. But the beautiful thing about it is that you can expect to see good results for your efforts even if you just allot 1-hour every day for posting quality content and developing your syndication strategy.

And even if you go for paid advertising on social media such as those of Facebook's and Twitter's, it can still be relatively cheap compared to traditional advertising media. The best way to keep your marketing costs low is to first start small, so you don't have to worry about exceeding your budget. So much of social media can be utilized with little or no monetary cost, and as we just saw, the time investment is reasonable. Increase your budget only when you get a better feel of how paid social media marketing actually works. Doing so can help increase your conversion rates.

BETTER SEO RANKINGS

The best way to direct traffic from search engines to your websites is still Search Engine Optimization or SEO. However, the requirements for successfully doing so continue to evolve. Today, updating your blog regularly, distributing links that lead back to your website, and optimizing your website's meta descriptions and title tags are no longer enough to ensure good rankings. But because the strongest product or service brands tend to rely heavily on social media for marketing and promotion, Google and other search engines may consider social media presence as one of those factors that weigh heavily in terms of ranking websites for certain keyword searches. There is, in fact, a plethora of evidence that supports the idea that

Google, Yahoo, Bing, and other search engines do in fact consider social media accounts when determining where your business will stand, so for that reason alone it's well worth creating and utilizing such services. If you'd like your business to rank well in keyword searches, you'll need to signal to search engines that your product or service is trustworthy, credible and legit. To do that, your business needs to be active on social media.

BETTER EXPERIENCE FOR CUSTOMERS

Social media is primarily a communications tool by nature, much like phone calls or emails. Every time you interact with a customer on social media, you have the opportunity to enrich your relationships with your current and existing customers by publicly demonstrating the high level of your customer service and giving them great experiences. This can be very evident in the way you handle complaints about your product or service on Facebook or Twitter. If you take immediate action to correct any errors, apologize publicly and address comments well, you communicate to the world that your product or service is worth their money is that you are very professional in serving your customers. This demonstrates the integrity of your business and even though having to apologize might seem negative, it is very likely to raise your prestige if handled correctly. Customers feel valued and important when their concerns or complaints are handled promptly and accurately, and social media allows you to prove to even still untapped customers that you are a business who can handle such things with dignity.

Another way you can give your customers better experiences to enrich your relationships with them is by acknowledging their compliments either by thanking them or recommending other useful products. Doing these two things, among others, gives your customers a great experience and let them know that you truly care about them. These simple steps illustrate for your customers how much you appreciate them and prove that you are willing to go the extra mile to ensure that they can obtain any other products they might desire.

OTHER THINGS TO CONSIDER

If you think that you really won't lose out on much if you don't utilize social media for your business, think again. For one, it's highly possible that your competitors are already using it for their advantage – over you! What this means is that the amount of potential traffic and corresponding conversions you can possibly tap may already be poached! In product or brand positioning, the pioneer normally has the upper hand.

And if your competitors aren't on social media yet, all the more you should beat them to the draw and establish your brands first and in the process, claim your marketing territory. In this case, not hasting leads to wasting – of opportunities.

Speaking of jumping the gun on your competitors, you'll reap more social media marketing benefits the sooner you get into it. Because social media is all about establishing and enriching relationships, your customer or marketing base can exponentially grow the more people tell others about your business on their social media accounts. The earlier you begin, the bigger your potential gains, business wise. A more immediate start means more customer loyalty is available- it is easier to gain customers who still need your products or services than it is to snatch them away from a competitor, no matter how good your business may be.

Lastly, if you're concerned with potential losses – don't be. It's because you can use social media marketing essentially for free! I mean, opening accounts and posting on Facebook, Twitter, Instagram and YouTube is free – at least the last time I checked. All that is required to utilize such networks is a small investment of your time- an investment that will almost certainly pay off as you gain more followers. And if you opt for paid social media advertising, you have great control over your budget as well as the demographic targets for your ads. Many such methods of advertising are at a very reasonable cost for the amount of people they can conveniently reach, and if you are comfortable reaching out to your target market in such ways you are likely to turn them into customers. As such, whatever costs you may incur with social media marketing can be substantially minimized.

So think about it – the more you put off social media marketing, the more benefits you pass out on. If you do it right, you can direct more people to your products or services and correspondingly, enjoy more conversions. Whether you believe it or not, social media – including marketing – is here to stay.

CHAPTER 3
GENERAL SOCIAL MEDIA MARKETING PRINCIPLES

Did you ever stop to think why practically everybody is on Facebook these days? Simple. It's because social media is fun.

But despite the relatively great amount of creative freedom social media platforms provide, you can't just be as lax and loose in using your business' social media pages as you do your personal ones. You'll have to develop an image, a persona, that you want to publicly present your business with, which can be a bit different than the live and let live sort of self-expression commonly found on personal accounts. For the purpose of increasing your chances of successfully marketing your products or services on social media, you'll need to keep in mind the following social media marketing principles.

ACT LIKE A PERSON

Since social media is...err...social, you need to be aware that nothing else can make your business anti-social than being too serious and projecting a robotic or mechanical image. In other words, a dead social media personality is – well – social media marketing death!

Therefore, you'll need to make your business' social media pages as social as possible by making it more like a personal account rather than a business one. But wait a minute – didn't I just say that you shouldn't use your business' social media accounts in a personal way? Yes, I did and what that meant was you don't take in as much liberty regarding posting whatever you want on them. Case in point: a critical comment.

With your business' social media page, you can't just bark at the person who gave a critical comment on the page or immediately disprove his or her claim, unlike in your personal account wherein you're very much free to do so. You'll have to respond to it in ways that keep the ethos that the customer is always right.

What I mean by making it more like a personal account is that you engage your customers and put content in ways that are alive and interesting. Instead of posting content that contains mostly facts and figures about your product, post content that illustrates how customers can benefit from using or availing your products or services. Instead of giving mere specs or product specifications, give examples, stories or testimonies of particularly useful or beneficial specs. By utilizing this method, you can make your business seem more personable and less business and goal oriented. This makes you seem more friendly, approachable, and trustworthy- all traits that increase the likelihood that you will gain first awareness, and then, increasingly, conversions.

TWO IS BETTER THAN ONE

While inbound marketing can significantly benefit your business, it's good to keep in mind that it's better if you augment it with some amount of outbound marketing, if practical and applicable. While inbound marketing refers to any type of marketing activity that seeks to draw or bring customers in towards your business, outbound marketing refers to marketing activities where you go out of your way to where the clients are, which include paid print advertisement or cold calling. Our ability to embrace this newfound technology can reap significant benefits for your business, but that is no reason to completely discard the older methods. If you take advantage of all options available, you can seamlessly blend the old and the new in order to attract the greatest amount of potential clients to your business.

IT'S ALL ABOUT THE CONTENT

As mentioned earlier, the secret to successful social media marketing campaigns is engagement. Your business websites' visits are important only to the extent that they provide opportunities to engage people with your products or services. Even if you have leads, they'll just go cold if you don't engage them.

And when it comes to successfully engaging your prospects, nothing else can be more helpful than providing high quality and unique content. Such content can steer readers to think about or even provoke them to give their two cents worth either by commenting on the content, liking it or sharing it with others. If you can master the art of getting your readers to take such actions, they are effectively promoting your content and your business for you, which is a surefire way to gain new customers and ensure the continued loyalty of the old. As such, content is truly king.

It can also pay to follow trends. While content always needs to be high quality and engaging, spur of the moment ideas passed on what is current and fresh can be pulled off to great effect with a bit of effort. Monitor what goes on in the news and what would be relevant to your industry and target market, and be sure to seize the opportunity to present spontaneous content when a good moment arises. This will show your consumers that you are modern, technologically savvy, and up to date on events and trends going on around us. In doing so, the content you post will seem new and interesting, and will, therefore, make potential customers want to look into it more than they otherwise might. Do be cautious when referencing current events, though. While witty or informative comments that promote your brand can be very compelling and entertaining, it would behoove you to learn from the mistakes of others and avoid referencing tragedies and other devastating events in a light hearted, good natured manner. When a mishap like this occurs, it can, depending on the severity, go viral, and that makes for very negative publicity. If this should happen to your business at any time, the best thing you can usually do is apologize and ensure your clients that such a mistake will not happen again. But with a bit of foresight, you can ensure content that is likely to be viewed as insensitive is simply never posted to begin with. At the end of the day, always be sure your posts are respectful and well thought out to avoid having to recover from such a travesty in the first place.

TELL THEM WHAT TO DO

An important part of engaging your customers is by giving a call to action, which is simply a direction or instruction that you give your customers or audience in order to provoke a quick response from them. Normally, calls to action use imperative verbs like "click here to find out more" or "download this program now."

In order to say that you've successfully engaged your prospects, you need to provide a call for action to give them an idea how you'd like them to engage back apart from simply sharing or liking your content, though you can certainly encourage them to do that, too! At the end of the day, customers want to be engaged. It makes them feel important, and, frankly, it can be fun. But if you do not provide them with any clear direction, they may lose interest. Exciting and stimulating instructions will ensure your clients are eager to follow them, and will raise the odds of them coming back for more. And because the ultimate goal of social media marketing is to help increase sales, calls to action are a very important part of it.

GIVE MORE

If you're honest with yourself, you'll agree that all of us do things primarily because we expect to get something out of them. Even for the seemingly noble and generous acts of the giving to or volunteering for good causes. It's because, in those cases, we still expect to get something, like self-fulfillment or the joy of knowing we've helped other people. At the end of the day, even acts that seem selfless usually are not due to the intangible but altogether selfish things we gain from them on a personal level.

According to Anthony Robbins, there are only two reasons that compel us to do the things that we do: pleasure and pain. Simply put, we do things because we crave pleasure, or we want to avoid pain. As such, you need to give your prospect something to make them come back to you for more and hopefully, engage your services, or buy your products. To engage them, you need to give them true value. If you don't, the chances of them coming back will be very low, and your leads will start to grow cold. Your clients have to gain pleasure with each visit and with each product or service purchased or utilized. If they feel the value or quality was poor, the level of pain they feel rises and the pleasure is diminished. You have to ensure your business is a fun and enticing place for your customers to visit, and enable them to enjoy their purchases to keep them coming back for more.

It can also help increase your views and followers if you make your content accessible and convenient to read or look at while on the go. With so many people accessing social media via smartphones, tablets, or other portable, handheld devices these days, ensuring they can comfortably enjoy your posts and contributions from any location can give you a slight step up over competitors who failed to consider such aspects.

IT'S A 2-WAY STREET

Social media marketing is basically a relationship process. And as I keep mentioning over and over again, it's about engagement. And this requires establishing relationships. Relationships require 2-way communications to flourish. If communication is just 1-way, you'll fail to really engage your customers. To truly qualify as engagement, you need to talk to your customers and allow them space and freedom to talk back to you, as opposed to just talking at them. If you do the former, more conversions are likely- the latter will result in eventual dismissal of your business as people feel bored or belittled when they do not get the opportunity to express themselves. Additionally, be prepared to acknowledge and respond to comments that criticize your business. If a customer feels wronged or short-changed in some way, they are likely to be quite vocal about it online, even if it's a minor complaint. Try to own up to any shortcomings and to make things right for your customers publicly. This will cause you to appear humble and humanize your company. If you are ready and able to handle criticisms, your target audience will gain respect for you and your conversions will increase.

One way that you can establish 2-way communications is by responding sincerely and promptly to any concerns that customers post on your product or service's social media pages. Another way to make it a 2-way street is to keep your content from sounding as if you're talking down on people. Instead, your content should encourage conversations with customers. Avoiding phrases such as "you will", "you must" and "you should" and replacing them with such words as "we should", "we must" and "we will" can go a long way in striking up 2-way conversations with your customers because the word "we" is more engaging and inclusive compared to the word "you". "We" ensures that your business and your clients are presented as a unified team. It eliminates the commanding nature of "you" phrases, which people intrinsically rebel against, and makes them feel a sense of comradery with your business. It enables your customers to feel like their voices are being heard and allows them to feel as though they are a valued and important part of your business.

It is important to realize that social networking is effectively joining a community. It's friendlier and more inclusive than standard methods of advertising could ever allow for, and puts businesses and customers in more direct contact with an equal footing. Treat your customers as though you care about them as individuals and as an intimate circle of those you care for, and they will respect and care for your company in turn. Reciprocity is a major component of social media.

UNDERSTANDING SEARCH ENGINE OPTIMIZATION

Search engine optimization is not what it used to be. Gone are the days of simply using a few choice words and soaring to the top of search results. These days, search engine optimization is vastly more complex than in previously years due to the massive increase in websites all vying for highly coveted spots. Back then, when the term first came to be in 1997, it was a very easy thing to abuse by way of stuffing irrelevant keywords into every page, thus tricking the search engines into displaying your company's page even if it made little to no sense considering the nature of the search. It was a cheap and easy marketing ploy, but it was hardly to the benefit of the customers or internet users as a whole, and the years have flown by since then and the entire way search engine optimization is formulated has been altered substantially. It is in fact so complicated these days that we will only touch on the tip of the iceberg here, but I highly suggest you research this topic in more depth as you delve ever deeper into the online world we are all living in now.

These days, unlike in the past, most major search engines, the most notable being Google, track the sites visited and searches made of every person who searches via their engine. It then generates websites, based on keywords and other factors, that each individual user is most likely to appreciate- custom designed results, leading to no two people receiving the exact same order of list as was the case in the past. You can use this feature to your advantage by knowing your target market well. Who are they, and what are their interests? With some research on the matter, and time getting to know your audience well, you can increase your chances of landing closer to the top.

It is important to note that, while previously it was common for businesses to carefully nurture their websites over a period of months or years to rank very highly, nowadays, thanks to Google Instant, search engines attempt to show fresh, recent, relevant results. This ensures that new posts and news articles will be forefront, which is exactly what most consumers desire. It does you no good to see the same old content again and again, after all. Additionally, there are now measures in place that penalize websites that copy the content of other websites- as such, always make your content fresh. Plagiarism does not pay off. Social media hits, followers, and activity can increase your ranking in search engine optimization calculations these days, though, making it yet another reason to choose a few platforms and begin marketing in this newfound manner right away.

While it is wise to have a basic understanding of search engine optimization in order to increase traffic to and interest in your site and by association your business, there are some disadvantages to investing a substantial amount of time and money into mastering it. Search engine optimization is a constantly changing system. According to Eric Schmidt, the CEO of Google, they made an average of 1.5 changes to their algorithm in 2010 alone, and these changes can very much influence where your company will rank. Imagine how devastating it would be to painstakingly work your way to the top of the rankings, investing a significant amount of time and money into it, only to fall back again only a day later. These days simply understanding search engine optimization is not enough. Is it helpful to understand, though? Certainly. But in the modern world we live in we are offered more reliable options, and doing the bulk of our marketing using the plethora of platforms offered to us by social media services is one of those options.

GETTING THE MOST OUT OF SOCIAL MEDIA

If you are worried about not using social media well enough to make a difference and you are daunted by the seemingly endless technological advances, you are not alone when it comes to breaking into the world of social media. There are a number of tools available to aid you in accomplishing precisely that. So many options exist these days to ensure your content is ready for your adoring public. There are a variety of tools that will assist you in a number of different categories, some of which we will discuss.

If you need help with managing your time, a task that can be rather overwhelming when you first dive into the endless sea of social media, you can find tools that remember passwords and account names, consolidate your applications, and help to enable you to manage your networking and marketing quickly and efficiently.

Need to make your pictures look prettier for Pinterest, Tumblr, Instagram, or any other social media account? There are programs out there that will give you the tools you need to expertly edit your photos, including but not limited to correcting flaws or imperfections, adjusting the appearance of lighting, or adding a variety of visually striking filters that might create just the mood you are looking to accomplish. It is worth noting, of course, that Instagram, unlike most similar social media sites (Pinterest and Tumblr included), includes the option to add filters. This system is fully integrated into the platform and can make for a very smooth experience, but if you would like to try your hand at further editing or prefer to focus on a different platform than Instagram, it can be valuable to gather some tools to ensure your images are presented in their most appealing form.

There are also tools and applications that enable you to track trends and analyze views and search results. This can, over time, better prepare you to determine what your target market is searching for, what content interests them and tugs at their heart strings, and ultimately, what they want to spend their time doing. This in turn allows you to customize your own content based on this data to ensure you are adequately providing what your clients want and need from you, leading to more conversions over time.

Keep in mind that most of these tools are free, so there is no reason not to take full advantage of them. It is important to note, of course, that they are widely available to individual users as well as businesses, so keep in mind that many of your potential customers will use them as well. If you consider how these applications benefit your clients as well as yourself, you can no doubt reap the benefits of them effectively.

CHAPTER 4
SOCIAL MEDIA MARKETING NO-NOS

While it's true that social media marketing provides or even requires a lot of creative freedom, it doesn't mean that everything we do is good for it. In this chapter, we'll take a look at some of the most common social media mistakes marketers commit for you to avoid them on your own campaigns.

LACKING PROFILES

Incomplete social media profiles, especially those used for businesses, give customers the impression that the business and its owners are either lazy or aren't competent enough to complete them. Regardless, it gives businesses bad publicity and PR.

An incomplete profile can destroy a business' reputation or integrity within the minds of its prospects even if the business is legitimate and thriving. It's because the social media page is just about the only point of reference they have at that point. Remember, it's true that first impressions last and as such, ensure that your business' social media account profile is complete before going live with it. Customers are unlikely to search for more information and may outright dismiss your business entirely if your accounts appear incomplete or inactive. They are trying to figure out what your company is about and how it might benefit them, and they won't much care to investigate further if your business profiles are inadequate.

NOT CONSISTENT

Especially if you use several different social media accounts to market your products and services, you have to make sure that all your social media accounts work together as a team and are consistent in terms of strategy, message and theme in order to project successfully and reinforce your desired image to the public. One example of being consistent is having the same user or account name and profile pictures for all social media accounts, whenever possible. Doing so establishes your products or services in your prospects' and customers' consciousness. It also subtly tells them that you're professional and put a great deal of attention to what you're doing. If such information varies it could lead to confusion on whether or not you are even the same company, and most people dislike being confused. Additionally, it could make you look dishonest or untrustworthy- both highly negative when trying to gain new clients.

NO PLANS

It's been said that failing to plan is planning to fail. It's no different when it comes to your social media marketing campaigns. A social media marketing campaign without a plan or strategy is like a car that's running, backed out of the garage and with no destination. Both are total wastes of precious resources.

What's worse is that conducting a social media marketing campaign without a plan or strategy can actually hurt your brand. This is because your brand doesn't stand a chance in terms of being noticed or single out from among the competition if it doesn't have a solid and well thought of strategy or plan. And inconsistency or poorly executed campaigns will give prospects the impression that you suck and consequently, that your brand sucks. Negative attention can be worse than no attention at all, as it can cost you even the customers you previously had the loyalty of if things are presented too poorly.

Plan accordingly!

BRAGGING

There's a big difference between promoting your products or services and bragging. When it comes to social media marketing, it's better to be a thought leader instead of an audacious self-promoter, which turns people off more than draw them in.

You can avoid the tendency to brag by always thinking of ways on how to construct your posts so that they give value to the readers instead of how to make your products or services look good. When you shift your focus from your products or services to the prospects' and customers' needs, you subtly communicate to them that you care about them and are very much interested in helping them out instead of just promoting your products and services and running away with their money. Focusing on them- instead of on yourself, your business, and your bottom line- makes them feel respected and valued, and in turn will cause them to respect and value you and your products, ultimately resulting in more conversions and more profit for your growing business.

PURE ADS

Unlike traditional or industrial marketing, social media is significantly less direct. Unlike traditional marketing that is focused solely on promoting a particular product or service, social media marketing is first and foremost all about engaging customers and prospects. Sales are just a byproduct or a bonus of the engagement process.

If you set up your social media pages to look more like eye-catching online advertisements, chances are very low that you'll be able to engage customers and prospects with unique and quality content. As such, you won't be able to provide them with great value to make them want to patronize your product or service. So always ensure that you post only unique, quality and useful content for your prospects and customers on your social media pages. Make your content fun. Make it thought provoking. Make it engaging. Do something different from the standard sales pitch to raise awareness of your company and you'll attract and maintain positive attention from potential customers, plus, they'll be more inclined to remember and recommend you if you do something outside the norm of standard advertising.

PURE WORDS

The primary way we communicate with each other is through words. But if we use pictures, will be able to paint a thousand words in just one sitting. And with all the information overload to which your prospects and customers are subjected to every day, there is but limited time and space to pitch your product and services to them. Many people lack the time, the patience, or both to sift through endless blocks of text. An interesting, compelling, or amusing picture will better catch and hold the attention of potential customers and motivate them to deem the words you do include, to be worth reading.

Because pictures paint thousands of words, nothing else works better than a picture or image that clearly communicates the message that you'd want your audience to receive. Another reason why you should include pictures in your posts is that scientifically speaking, our brains think in pictures. This is the principle behind the term "photographic memory". Your future customers will better remember and therefore think about your business and products if you utilize images and photos instead of simply words. If you use images or pictures wisely and strategically, you can position your product or services in the minds of your customers and prospects more effectively.

TAKING #HASHTAGS FOR GRANTED

When you see phrases or words that are preceded by the # sign, you're looking at hashtags. These are used to put certain content under particular online conversations or topics. Using hashtags is a good way for you to place your product or services into mainstream, online trending topics or conversations. If you use hashtags wisely and strategically, you can narrow down your target market, thereby widening your potential customer base from which you can get solid leads. You can include some diverse hashtags on any given post, so be sure to include all applicable ones that your target market might have an interest in. This will ensure your comments and posts are seen with more searches than ever before, widening their visibility and therefore that of your company. It's free and takes up almost no time, so it's well worth investing a minute or two to ensure more publicity.

INCLUDING URLS IN POSTS

Many people make the mistake all of including the URLs of links that they post on social media, particularly Facebook. Normally, this happens because after putting a link, a clickable image is created, which makes users forget that the URL is still on the post.

While including the URL in your post is not a sinful or evil act in social media marketing contexts, it may affect your product's or service's reputation by sending the message that the people behind your products and services - including you - aren't well versed with social media and can make your product or service look inferior compared to those of your competitors'. This could lead to potential customers thinking you are technologically behind, uncool, or unprofessional. It might also make them less likely to recommend or like your posts if they include URLs or other such errors that cause your business to appear less eye-catching and more behind the times. It's better to err on the side of caution and as such, ensure that you always remove URLs from your social media posts.

ONE WAY, JOSE

Because social media is social, as the name suggests, it is intended to facilitate interaction. Your customers and prospects will ask to expect a good amount of interaction from you on social media.

In order to make your customers and prospects feel a good sense of connection with your products or services, its best to respond sincerely, politely, courteously and promptly to your followers comments or posts on your page.

Don't be caught unprepared. Always have ready and well-thought guidelines for responding to all your followers' comments – positive or negative – and plans of action for managing potential crisis situations. A prompt and respectful response to a negative comment can work wonders for mending ties and building bridges, and witty banter, warm words, and friendliness will take you far when responding to positive or neutral comments. Be informative to queries and communicative to even the smallest comments- your customers will feel included, and their appreciation will show in your profits.

NOT ENOUGH CONTENT

A common mistake those starting out with social media marketing are guilty of, when all intentions are good, is simply not posting enough. It is easy to start out strong on your platform of choice, posting at least once a day, maybe several times, and then become discouraged if you do not have many views, likes, and shares very quickly. This can lead to despairing or burning out, which can cause you to slack on posting any new content, or doing so very infrequently. Like most good things, it takes time to gain followers, so do not give in to defeat if you do not results right away- multiple studies show us time and time again that these strategies are successful, so keep at it! Additionally, sometimes well-meaning business owners or managers start social media accounts and simply are too busy or overwhelmed to find the time to post. In this situation, if budget allows for it, it might make sense to hire someone to oversee your social media accounts and to serve as the persona of your business. If finances do not allow for such, simply set a reasonable goal for yourself. It might be recommended to make several posts a day, but even just one will work wonders for your company. Start with something you can manage and commit to ensuring you can adequately respond to and engage with your customers and potential customers. You can always post more content when and if time permits it.

CHAPTER 5

THE RIGHT SOCIAL MEDIA PLATFORM FOR YOUR BUSINESS

Alright. Now that you decided to promote your business better by giving social media marketing a try, which social media platform should you use? Should you use all, just a few or many?

Social media is very much like your social life: it can be rewarding, awkward, confusing, demanding or even fun. Many people believe that social media is a very valuable resource but at the same time, great care needs to be exercised in terms of managing the amount of resources and time invested in it. With the sheer number of available social media channels on the Internet today, you may be tempted to simply raise up your hands and ditch the whole idea of social media marketing. Too many choices have been shown time and again to be overwhelming, which can make it hard to choose anything at all. But you don't really have a choice. If you want to keep your business growing and increase sales and profits, you will need to use social media. Which forms of social media you select and how many of them you manage are, of course, entirely up to you, but choose wisely. It is important to consider the networks your target markets will be most active on in order to maximize your time and resources on those social media platforms firstly.

Do you remember how your parents used to remind about choosing your friends wisely when you were still a kid? Keep that advice in mind as you employee social media marketing for your business. With all the available social media platforms out there, it's important to choose only the best social media sites for running your marketing campaigns in order to maximize your limited social media time and resources. Certainly utilizing many, if not all, of the available resources and networks may seem ideal at first glance, but I warn you to look again. While we discussed that social media management does not take too long to see a profit, there is a point of diminishing returns and how much time and budget you have available for such endeavors. Investing no time or finances will reap no reward, but investing too much will leave you tired and drained and worn too thin. As such I advise you to focus only on the social media platforms most likely to raise awareness within your target audience and net you eventual conversions.

So instead of just blindly following the social media crowd, it's better if you approach it the same way you chose your hangout spots when you were still in high school: Where do the folks with the same interests as me hang out?" The more familiar you become with using social media, you will start to realized that the term "cool" or "relevant" is subjective and could mean different things for different people.

So when it comes to social media marketing, you need to know your prospects and customers as well as their interests. Then finally, you must narrow down your choices of social media platforms to use based on which networks they'll probably gravitate to. If you are targeting primarily middle-aged men, you'll be looking into entirely different networks than if you are aiming to catch the attention of twelve year old girls. Plan poorly and you are sure to be disappointed. Plan well and reap the financial and prestige awards that come with watching your business grow and develop.

Here are some of the most popular social media platforms on the Internet today and for whom such platforms are most beneficial.

FACEBOOK

If your primary goal is to reach the broadest network possible or if you're just starting out in terms of building your products' or services' presence, then Facebook may be the social media platform for you. While it has been losing its grip among the younger users, a staggering 70% of adults who regularly go online still actively participate in this social media platform, making it the most popular one as of today. And more than just having the most number of users, Facebook is also the one with the highest level of engagement as evidenced by it being the most frequently used social media site. So many people of many diverse age groups, from teenagers and even children on up through senior years of life, utilize Facebook on a near daily basis. Many of them also spend hours each day invested into their Facebook lives- be it playing games, chatting, or simply browsing things they and their friends "like", Facebook has become an active social hub that can be an excellent place to reach a very wide audience and to get your foot in the door if you are still small and need to spread some general awareness of your business goals and products.

One possible limitation or drawback to using Facebook for social media marketing is that people use Facebook primarily to connect with friends, family, and colleagues. Since engagement is the primary objective for most Facebook users, it may not necessarily be the most effective social media platform to promote your products or services. A potential way to limit this drawback exists if you can master the art of presenting your company in a friendly, homey sort of manner. Something that makes people feel comfortable and relaxed might allow you to better work your way into their social circles and connect with them on a more personal level than could otherwise be accomplished. The diversity and ubiquity offered by Facebook make it a good starting point well worth considering- but hardly the only option that social media has to offer you.

LINKEDIN

If you're in the industry of providing helpful insights to people who are looking for jobs, looking to expand their business networks or connections and evaluating or thinking about their careers, then LinkedIn may be the social media platform that's right for you. It's also a good choice if you're in the B2B (business-to-business) market.

LinkedIn is best for industry specific information and peer networking although it's trying to expand its information scope as of the moment. Because the average LinkedIn user enjoys high income and education levels, it can provide you with a distinct target market that's worth going after using the right message. LinkedIn manifests a more professional image and a more professional goal- it is far more common to see people chatting or gaming with friends over Facebook than LinkedIn, but that does not lessen LinkedIn's value. It allows connections within the professional world, be that finding employees or contacting other businesses, in a way unmatched by the other social media platforms on this list, and it offers you a specific demographic that may well be exactly the market you are trying to reach.

PINTEREST

If you're in the business that's highly visual and if your customers and prospects are the types of people who express themselves naturally through pictures or images, then Pinterest may be the right social media platform for your business. Even if the nature of the business you're in doesn't look visual at first, Pinterest may still work for you.

Consider the interests of your prospects and customers. Do they like collecting pictures and images in order to get information concerning the products or services they're considering buying or availing? Are they greatly interested in things that can be represented visually? It can work well for more than what is traditionally thought of as art, though it is no doubt an excellent platform to select if you are marketing pictures, paintings, or other traditional art choices. Anything within the realm of fashion, be it clothing, shoes, jewelry, or makeup, does phenomenally well on Pinterest. In that same spirit interior and/or exterior design and building companies, including furniture, paint, decorating services, or architecture businesses can thrive on Pinterest. It can also be an excellent platform to promote restaurants, coffee shops, bars, or other food or beverage type establishments, as getting a visual can tempt and entice your potential patrons. It even works well for less intuitive business models, like gyms or personal trainers- a visual representation of the workouts and equipment can really help with motivation. Pinterest can be a fantastic tool for any product or service with a strong visual component, and, with a little bit of outside the box thinking, may very well prove successful for a great many other services.

It's also worth noting that Pinterest is greatly popular among women, so it's a good social media platform for promoting feminine products as well. A large part of making social media marketing work well for you is knowing where to find your customers, and so the demographics you find can prove important information when selecting your platform (or platforms!) of choice.

INSTAGRAM

As with Pinterest, Instagram may be the right social media platform for your business if your products, services, and customers are highly visual. As such, it can make an excellent alternative choice to Pinterest, or you can use them in tandem to reach a broader audience. It's interesting to note that Instagram and Twitter users often overlap and as such, Instagram can be used as a good part of a double-edged social media marketing sword.

Instagram is a very good social media marketing platform for targeting market niches particularly because it appeals to particular ethnic segments and is popular among people who live in urban areas.

TWITTER

While it limits you to 140 character tweets at a time, Twitter has a very large network of diverse followers and can be an excellent social platform to use to market your business. By using hashtags well and tweeting witty or informative comments, you can gain quite the following. You can also share images and other content via Twitter and encourage your followers to retweet or favorite what you share, even tying such actions to promotions when prudent.

In spite of the limitation on word amount, Twitter can be an eye-catching tool that will attract even the potential clients who might have otherwise not noticed your business, and with around three hundred million users, it's an option well worth considering.

YOUTUBE

Youtube focuses primarily on videos and other media clips. As such, you can present a very successful marketing campaign via compelling and entertaining videos you create. Keep them relatively brief and ensure that they are catchy lest you lose the attention of your viewers.

Youtube receives millions of visitors each month, many of whom watch for several hours each visit. It has also been around for ten years now, ensuring a wide age range to target. Keep in mind that certain topics and products are quite polarized by gender, though- name and market your videos according to what group or groups you decide to market to.

GOOGLE+

Google+ is a bit different from most other social media platforms in that it is, more or less, simply the social component of Google's many tools and services. Using Google+, you can create or join a community in which you can share posts and content and view that which is posted and shared by others within your community.

Google+ is predominantly male. According to statisticsbrain.com, about 74% of it's 400,000 active users are men, many of them within the fields of web and computer development or engineering. Currently, only about 40% of marketers use Google+, making it a potentially untapped territory within your field. In spite of being smaller in the sheer number of users than most of the other platform choices we've discussed, it is growing by about 33% each year, making it a possibly strong emerging candidate that might be well worth your attention.

TUMBLR

Tumblr is a mini blogging platform with heavily dominated by visual media. Pictures, images, videos, and gifs, preferably animated ones, are the primary tools of choice on Tumblr. A humorous or distinctive name can be a good bet on Tumblr as it is likely to be appreciated by the people using it.

The majority of Tumblr users are young, hip individuals at the forefront of new trends and ideas. Emerging technology, trending fashions, and other up and coming products are likely to thrive in this environment. It is close to being equally split between young men and young women, so you can readily target either or both genders depending on your business and ideal audience.

NOW, MAKE THAT CHOICE(S)

Now that you have an idea about some of the most popular social media platforms out there, it's time to make the choice or choices. This means looking for your customers and going to where they are using the right kind of content, whether it's original or shared from sports, entertainment, news and other sources that can be trusted.

It's also entails being realistic concerning what you can do and how much you can do in terms of engaging or interacting with customers. After all, social media is a reciprocal channel that requires you to participate in conversations that are relevant and sensible to your business and customers. You must learn to prioritize the conversations that make the most sense to the needs of your clients, and of course, to your own needs as a company. No one has enough time to sift through everything ever posted on social media, and no customer would expect such a level of dedication from you- but try to ensure you communicate promptly and respond to anything relevant, to lessen the chances of your customers feeling ignored or unappreciated. Social media should accomplish quite the opposite of that, and with a bit of time and effort on your part, it will.

CHAPTER 6

FACEBOOK MARKETING

There's no question that Facebook is the biggest social media platform in the history of mankind. If you don't believe me, consider these statistics culled from statisticbrain.com as 20 September 2015:

- Total number of monthly active Facebook users: 1,440,000,000

-Total number of mobile Facebook users: 874,000,000

-Increase in Facebook users from 2014 to 2015: 12 %

-Total number of minutes spent on Facebook each month: 640,000,000

-Percent of all Facebook users who log on in any given day: 48 %

-Average time spent on Facebook per visit: 18 minutes

-Total number of Facebook pages: 74,200,000

Any objections? I rest my case.

However way you put it, the above-mentioned figures represent a LOT of people! And naturally, where there are many people, there are many prospects. And guess what? More prospects equal more business opportunities! Additionally, Facebook offers tremendous diversity, featuring potential customers of all ages, backgrounds, and lifestyle choices, enabling you to reach your target market successfully. No matter who you are trying to reach or what you are trying to sell, you can find the appropriate clients on Facebook.

WHY IT MAKES SENSE

Of course, we're not saying all 1 billion+ users are your actual prospects or potential customers. Many of the active Facebook members will be far from the market you are seeking. But what such the statistics imply is that in terms of exposure, there's no better place on the Internet for marketing than Facebook. But this is just the tip of the so-called social media marketing iceberg. Let's take a look at other reasons why marketing on Facebook makes so much sense.

Segments

Here's a very interesting piece of useful information: Facebook keeps a vast database on just about everything and anything related to its users. Favorite things, location, age, likes, interests and more... check! So what's the point?

There are two ways to advertise your products and services on Facebook: free and paid. The information available in Facebook's database is particularly useful for paid advertising. Why is that so?

Traditional advertising like radio, TV or print ads uses a shotgun approach – i.e., mass advertising where you simply hope there's enough of your target audience to watch, hear or read your advertisement. But with Facebook, you have the ability to target specific market for your paid advertisements.

For example, your business is an Italian restaurant located in Nebraska. Further, yours is a rather eccentric one that plans to cater specifically to people who love Italian food and who worship the late David Bowie. You can advertise your restaurant on Facebook and filter your advertisements to target users who live in Nebraska, who love David Bowie and worship Italian food. But considering Nebraska's quite a large area, you can further narrow down your target audience to those living in Norfolk!

Another example – say you're a freelance author who specializes in personal finance. You can market your e-books on Facebook using paid advertisements to target people between the ages of

20 to 30 years who are interested in learning how to invest for their future. If you're rather chauvinistic and would like to limit it to male audiences, you can instruct Facebook to show your advertisements to men only. It's that specific, which is not even remotely possible with traditional media. It is this specificity that enables social media marketing to shine in ways previously unheard of. By targeting the exact demographic you are looking for, all the way down to interests and location, you are securing the best possible odds of increasing your sales exponentially and enabling your business to develop in ways once impossible.

Cost Management

You can easily limit your advertising spending when conducting Facebook marketing campaigns. This is because you can control not just the maximum amount you're willing to spend for such campaigns but also how long such campaigns will last and how much of your budget to spend every day.

For example, you only have a maximum budget of $30 for a 30-day Facebook marketing ad campaign. Facebook will automatically limit your spending to $1 per day over the next 30 days to keep you within your budget. As such, you don't have to worry about runaway spending. This enables you to start with advertising within your reach, no matter where your business is financially and expand your marketing campaigns when and if you have the ability and desire without having to stress about the money invested in it.

MARKETING ON FACEBOOK

If you want to maximize your market reach as well as Facebook's features, you'll need to understand some of the best Facebook marketing practices. While these aren't necessarily hard and fast rules, following these practices can significantly improve your product or service's ability to engage customers on Facebook.

And remember what I kept on repeating earlier, that social media marketing is primarily about engagement? If you go out and study the Facebook pages of many of the world's most popular brands, one glaring thing you'll notice is that they hardly ever sell directly to followers nor do they preach to them. Instead, they engage.

It also happens that people are a lot more intelligent these days such that they can immediately smell if you're just trying to sell to them or if you're sincerely and genuinely engaging them. Always keep in mind that Facebook is a social network first and foremost, and it's not sales and marketing network. People want friendliness, respect, and inclusion- they are on Facebook to socialize and to have fun, not to repeatedly listen to and ultimately reject ill-advised sales pitches. Engage them, involve them, and they will reward you for it. Give them a generic advertisement and watch your prospects fizzle. The choice here is clear.

Thomas Meloche and Perry Marshall, in their book Ultimate Guide to Facebook Advertising, discussed how different Facebook marketing is from traditional advertising, whether it's online or on print, by using a front porch story or analogy, which goes something like this:

> *Imagine a town square and you live in that area. Imagine further that your house features a front porch where you enjoy watching people pass and cultivate many beautiful plants. There days when you're enjoying watching people pass by and drinking from a pitcher of cold lemonade that some of those people notice your front porch's beautiful plants and approach you to ask how you keep them looking beautiful.*
>
> *You offer them seats on your porch and give them glasses of cold lemonade while explaining the general principles for keeping your plants beautiful and healthy. Some of those people become so interested in plant cultivation because of your sharing that they'd be willing to spend money just to have a day with you and learn the finer details of how you grow and keep plants beautiful. You take them up on their offer and spend the next day teaching them how you do it.*

In that example, did you observe any explicit or direct attempts to sell anything on your porch? How about any implicit attempts to promote a horticulture seminar? That's right, none! And in a nutshell, that's how you do Facebook marketing. Any selling is done only within the framework of relationships and personal connections.

As I always say, it's about engagement. A very good way for you to engage people on Facebook is by posting helpful tips or links to articles that they'll like and share as well as by asking relevant questions. When your posts focus on your audience, their needs, and their interests, you develop relationships, which is the single biggest reason for the existence of social media. People want to view you, more or less, as another of their friends. It pays to talk to them accordingly. Helpful tips on things they might want or need is great, upselling them things is not. Focus on your customer's happiness over your own success, and you'll wind up fulfilling both goals. And as the preceding porch story has shown, sales can just be a result of such relationships.

Another great way to engage your prospects and customers on Facebook is by consistently posting unique and quality content every day. Although it may seem quite cumbersome to do it at such frequency because of very busy schedules, posting such content less frequently increases the risk of your target audience missing some of your important posts because over time, they tend to follow and like more and more Facebook pages. And these "new" likes and follows will compete for their social media attention and engagement. When they miss more of your posts and see more of others', their interest in yours starts to dwindle and in others to increase – and there goes your prospects and sales leads. If you are short on time, keep in mind that such posts don't have to be long. Aim to make them eye catching and interesting. Try to include content that stands out amongst a sea of other posts, no matter how daunting that may seem. Keep in mind the interests of your target audience- your posts certainly won't sway everyone on Facebook, but they don't have to for you to succeed. Catch and hold the attention of the customers you want with attentive engagement and quality posts and you'll have loyal clients for as long as you maintain your activity.

Several studies recommend posting 3 to 5 times daily on Facebook for optimal engagement with prospects and customers. However, each and every situation is different and as such, I recommend that sensible and strategic experimentation to see which will work best for your business. Make a goal that works for you, be it once a day or ten times daily. Just aim to be consistent and post regularly to keep people looking forward to seeing what you have to say.

Lastly, you should keep your posts fun and interesting. Remember, a big chunk of successful engagement is having fun so keep your posts helpful, interesting and light as much as possible. No one wants to be overwhelmed with heavy, difficult content in their free time. Informative entertainment, ideally with pictures, videos, or other visually compelling additions makes for an ideal goal that will catch and hold the attention of your target market, leading to eventual conversions.

CHAPTER 7
TWITTER MARKETING

Based on a survey conducted by Ask Your Target Market, about 42% of people who use Twitter do so to follow companies or brands. And since you're a businessperson who is looking to market your business over social media, that's great news! Next only to Facebook, Twitter is the second largest social media site in terms of users with over 646 million users as of 25 September 2015, according to statisticbrain.com. And when you look at it, it's even larger than the population of most countries in the world. It offers a tremendously diverse and far-reaching group of people you can market to, and unlike the denizens of Facebook, many Twitter users actually want to be marketed to. As such, Twitter can be another excellent social media platform to market your products or services.

Compared to Facebook, Twitter is considered to be a micro-blogging website, i.e., you can only post updates that are at most 140 characters long. Initially, this limit was intended to make it compatible with most mobile phones and text messaging services. Since then, it has evolved into a somewhat useful and practical feature for sending and receiving concise and quick information among many people. This might make you feel restrained, but there is a lot you can do to gain attention, and you can say more than you'd imagine in 140 characters.

Using Twitter can help you market your product or services over social media by among other things:

-Developing productive relationships with bloggers and journalists for PR;

-Enhancing your industry expertise and thought leadership reputation;

-Promoting your product or service's upcoming activities or events;

-Helping you find out how people think and feel about your product or service;

-Engaging your product or service's customer base; and

-Growing your brand.

MARKETING ON TWITTER

You can use Twitter as a very powerful marketing tool to help direct more traffic to your business website, promote your business' activities and events, monitor economic activity and share your expertise. By inserting a link in your tweets, you drive people to your business website and promote any coupons or special offers, inform them of interesting developments on your product or service and provide them with access to very interesting and quality content. Fans may even re-tweet the things you share on Twitter if they find your content to be very good and unique, it multiplies or leverages the amount of traffic that can be directed to your business website and as such, you gain access to more marketing leads. You can gently and enthusiastically request that people take the time to retweet content they enjoyed, thus generating a higher amount of interest in your company and what you have to say, or, more precisely, what you have to tweet.

By using the "Connect" tab on your Twitter account, you can monitor your product or service's activities on Twitter. You can also do this by signing up for updates that are sent via email. Lastly, you can use software to get a closer look at all of your product or service's Twitter activities.

Word of mouth is one of the best ways to market a product or service. And testimonials are one of those ways that your business can be promoted by word of mouth. A very good way of collecting good testimonials for your product or service is by using Twitter's "Favorites" feature. Such testimonials are significant social proof for your product or service and can help enhance the image of your product or service, making it more popular. People are inherently social creatures, and if something is popular and well liked, they usually want to try it out as well. The more clients you have that favorite your business, the more positive reviews you will effectively hold. That will raise your reputation in the eyes of any social media consumer.

Using this feature is as easy as 1-2-3. You just hover over any tweet in your stream and then a list of options will appear, from which you can click "Favorite". Your product or services get more social proof as the number of favorite tweets contained in your tab increases. It's well worth favoring tweets your followers and potential customers share as well, particularly any that support or reference your business or similar things in any way. It shows clients that you are listening and interacting with them, and it makes them feel special.

One way you can promote or market your business' promotional activities – like campaigns, webinars or events – is by tweeting about it and inserting a link that will direct people to your event's sign up page. Oh, it's best that you come up with a very nice hashtag for your activity first before you even tweet about it. Including diverse and descriptive hashtags will ensure your tweets are present in a number of different categories and increase their visibility. Inappropriate use of or simply lacking of hashtags will lead to your tweets not getting much attention, and using them well is an easy, quick, and free method of directing more potential clients to your business.

You can help make your brand a preferred or leading one by tweeting useful resources and tips regularly. As you do this, it's best to tweet a good amount of both your original or owned resources and those of other people's. Apart from establishing your product or service leadership, it can also project an image that's humble and open. This makes you appear personable- almost human, yet also knowledgeable. A source that people can trust and depend upon is a resource they'll happily utilize.

When using Twitter, keep in mind that there are a number of tools and programs that you can use to maximize the time you spend and to ensure you gain the greatest amount of followers. Many of these work by making it easier for you to find people and companies to follow- and it helps you to notice when someone you once took an interest in becomes inactive so that you can unfollow. It's worth noting, of course, that many of your clients will use these tools as well, so strive to ensure your own activity does not fall too low, lest you disappoint them.

PUBLIC RELATIONS

Public relations is a very important part of any effective marketing campaign, traditional or modern (i.e., social media). One way to do this is by introducing your business and your products and services to those who can spread word about them far and wide – the media. Because many media people such as bloggers, reporters and journalists are also on Twitter, it only makes sense to use this micro-blogging site for effective public relations or PR.

One way to do this is by first following or subscribing to blogs that are most popular or well known in our particular industry or niche. From there, you can glean ideas as to which influential or beneficial Twitter authors or personalities to follow. You can also follow well-known journalists who cover your industry or niche and to tweet about their published works and get their opinions on industry or niche-related topics, which can help you get on their good side. Once you do, you can tweet them about your products or services, taking care not to "sell" them. Establishing such professionally personal relationships with influencers can go a long way in promoting your brands. In many cases, it will cost you nothing, and having powerful and influential friends like these effectively results in free advertising for you. Favorite and retweet what they say, get to know their thoughts and opinions on things, and your business will flourish as their endorsement will excite new potential customers into converting.

CHAPTER 8

MARKETING ON INSTAGRAM

As you may already know by now, Instagram is a social media website which lets its users edit, filter and share pictures and video to many other people over the Internet. It also allows users to simultaneously share these over Twitter, Facebook, Flickr and Tumblr. According to statisticbrain.com, Instagram has over 183 million registered users who have already shared more than 18 billion pictures and videos that garner an average of 1.65 billion likes daily as of 11 September 2015. If that's not big enough for you, I don't know what is!

Businesses have also started looking to Instagram to sell their brands, particularly because pictures (and videos) paint a thousand (and more) words, and our brains think better in pictures. These major businesses include G.E., Adidas, Virgin America, American Express, Intel and Red Bull, among many others.

Intel, for example, promotes their latest, cutting-edge processors via Instagram with pictures of the latest computer models that utilize them. More than just posting pictures on Instagram, they post highly creative pictures that make their otherwise "boring" products come to life with excitement. It features all sorts of technological wonders on its Instagram, including both widely available products as well as more eclectic but rapidly growing choices like the results of 3-D printing. Its Instagram account features a wide range of photos that paint different pictures as to how Intel's products continue to influence our way of life as we know it.

In contrast, the Instagram account of Virgin America is less creatively styled than most others. At one point, they used photos of the very popular Pomeranian puppy Boo in promoting their first class flights as dog-friendly over this social media site.

American Express promotes its financial services on Instagram, particularly by posting mostly photos of the many important events they've sponsored as well as by using #hashtags in promoting their products' image as those that are essential for modern living.

Keep in mind that while you can post short videos on Instagram, it's not optimal to do so. If you're gunning for video promotions, your best bet is still YouTube, which is designed primarily for uploading videos. Focus your resources on beautifully creative pictures and images on Instagram to optimize your use of this particular social media platform.

Posting pics on Instagram isn't as easy as snapping photos and uploading them – at least not for social media marketing purposes. Before you promote your products or services of this social media platform, consider your target audience, the optimal engagement strategy and what will provoke them into talking about your brand and photographs of them. When you know your audience well, you'll know the kinds of pictures that'll appeal to them. Instagram allows you to get truly creative with your marketing, enabling you to use it to advertise virtually any product. Once you get to know your customer base, design a beautifully well-pictured marketing campaign that will appeal to the audience you are trying to attract. When you know your audience well, you'll also be able to develop strategies that will get them to talk about your brand, which provides opportunities for engagement and consequently, brand awareness and promotion.

BEST PRACTICES

By also posting pictures of the people behind your products and services on Instagram, you "humanize" your business by allowing your followers to see the hands and faces behind the inanimate objects they are following on Instagram. Social media in all of its many forms depends, primarily, on connecting with our fellow human beings. Let your potential customers see you as you work, and witness the hands-on, emotional, relatable side of your business, as opposed to just the end result they so commonly see. Humanizing your products and services allows your followers to connect with your business on a deeper level and increases their chances of becoming hot leads and eventually, customers.

You can also draw in more prospects and leads by featuring pictures that show how your products are created and packaged or how your services are rendered. The point of doing this is to make your followers more familiar with your brand and as they become so, the more likely they can become leads and customers. If they understand more of how your process works from the start, they are more likely to trust and rely on your products and in doing so, they will become to rely on your business as well. Most people are naturally curious and knowing what goes into the creation of items they enjoy can make them feel more bonded to such items, as well as offering them reassurance that the methods you claim to use are every bit as ethical as you suggest, gaining you additional trust and loyalty. Just don't give too much "details" to prevent your competition from spying on you and undercutting you.

Lastly, use originally unique and catchy #hashtags, which is Instagram's most effective marketing tactic. Using such can help your brand become more visible to more people, which can lead to more prospects, leads and consequently sales.

CHAPTER 9

YOUTUBE MARKETING

Google owns this website that allows its users to upload, share, comment and watch videos. It's search engine is probably the 2nd biggest in the world next to its parent company and by far, the biggest video sharing website on the planet. As such, it's the best social media platform to use videos in promoting your products and services. But with so many videos uploaded and continue being uploaded on YouTube – about 72 hours' worth of video every minute being uploaded on the site – how can you effectively reach your target audiences?

The first thing you'll need to do is create your own "channel" on YouTube, which should neither be too difficult nor complicated. After you've done it comes the most challenging part, producing very compelling videos for upload.

So what makes for compelling videos? First, consider the content, which should engage your target customers within 15 seconds or less. Otherwise, your viewers will be bored and won't bother watching your videos long enough to appreciate it. This is because of the information overload they're all subject to each and every day. To really engage them within the first 15 seconds, use introductions that are animated and quick to both spark their curiosity and win their trust. This helps them expect something great from watching the video further.

Another important quality your videos need to have are calls to action – and this is key for any social media campaign to succeed. You can place the call to action at any point on the video, depending of course on its message. Just ensure you don't overdo your calls to action because for one, having too many such calls may confuse the viewers and as such, just keep your calls minimal and easy to understand and respond to. Some of the common and sensible calls of action to include in your videos are subscribing to your YouTube channel, commenting on your videos, liking-adding-sharing your videos and visiting your brand's official website and/or other social media platforms, among others.

And more than just compelling, you should also post videos on YouTube regularly to increase your presence in YouTube and consequently, increase the number of your subscribers. One way to ensure regularity is to create shorter videos of a particular long-form content, i.e., divide one long topic or video into series of shorter videos. Instead of producing a "movie", create shorter episodes that are not only easier to watch and understand but also spark more curiosity and interest. It can help if you release each new segment on a designated day and time, and remain consistent. Once you get people hooked on your channel, they'll be eagerly looking forward to watching your new video each time a new one is posted, and if you let them know when that will be, they'll incorporate your channel into part of their daily routine. Be careful to avoid sporadic or infrequent updates, though, or your followers are likely to grow bored and no longer anticipate further content, leading to less loyalty and fewer customers. Be consistent, and make it entertaining, and your current clients will recommend your videos to their friends, likely via social media itself.

VIDEO VISIBILITY

No amount of consistency in terms of posting high-quality and interesting videos on YouTube will ever make up for lack of visibility. After all, what good are videos – however excellent the content – if viewers can't find them? While this is more about search engine optimization (SEO), which is a very complicated topic to discuss here, you can do the following to improve your videos' visibility and allow more people to view it.

One is carefully written titles. Make sure that your videos' titles include targeted keywords in the first few ones and that they're followed by a colon (:) for optimal visibility. An example of this is a video on how to self-publish your first e-book with a video title "Self-Publishing Success: A Beginner's Guide".

Next are your videos' descriptions, which you'll need to begin with a full URL. You'll also need to provide as many details about the video as possible without giving away its main attractions or points so that people will still want to watch it. In other words, enough details without spoilers.

CHAPTER 10

LINKEDIN MARKETING

A social media site specifically created for business communities, LinkedIn's goal is to give its registered members the opportunities to build and establish documented professional networks of people that they know and trust. A typical profile page of LinkedIn's members prioritize or highlight working experience or history and education – 2 of the most important criterion by which people are evaluated in the business world for business partnerships or employment. The profile page also features a professional network news feed with several modules that can be customized.

Basically, membership is free, and members are referred to as "connections". Another basic difference between LinkedIn and social networking platforms like Facebook – aside from its business theme – is that LinkedIn requires that you have a pre-existing relationship with a prospective connection first before being connected. Many aspects of LinkedIn, including that one, are designed with a more professional, business oriented mindset than most other social networking sites, including Facebook, can boast, though of course that leads to less of the light-hearted social interactions that Facebook is full of. LinkedIn can be a valuable resource for connecting you with other business or with business professionals, and can be an ideal platform for targeting anyone within that demographic.

SOCIAL MEDIA MARKETING, LINKEDIN STYLE

Because this is all about building networks, what you're actually marketing on LinkedIn is yourself as an entrepreneur or business professional. Obviously, the more you market yourself professionally, the more business contacts you gain, which is only beneficial for your businesses in general.

So how do you market yourself well in LinkedIn? One way is to build up your profile of course! Since you're selling yourself, make yourself look good on it. LinkedIn isn't just about being sociable and engaging- major aspects of most other social networking sites. Here you can sell yourself, and your business, so don't be too shy or modest about your strengths. You can build your profile up in LinkedIn using the following features, among others:

-Status Updates: Short statements about you that you think your connections will find most interesting or useful. Here, you can include content-related links to other sites, including your business' own, as well as links to other relevant sites and your other social media accounts. Posting actionable and useful status updates regularly can make you look more active on LinkedIn. Activity will show motivation and work ethic and will go a long ways towards showing prospective connections how dedicated and professional you can be.

-Blog Posts: This site lets you effortlessly syndicate your profile with your blog posts and vice versa. What this means is you can allow your LinkedIn profile to update automatically with your blogs on your business' website by providing a link and abstract of such blogs.

-Presentations: You can also post slide presentations such as those of Google Docs, PowerPoint or SlideShare to your LinkedIn profile.

-Events: You can post events on your LinkedIn profile to promote events that you're either promoting, managing or conducting.

-Tweets: You can also connect your Twitter tweets to your LinkedIn status updates to better keep your connections and followers updated on your latest happenings.

You can also brand your LinkedIn address by customizing it. Much like a personal website, a branded LinkedIn address can help boost your professional image. Choose wisely- the address you select will represent your company. You'll want to appear professional and also select something well suited to what your business sells, offers, or represents.

Lastly, you can use LinkedIn's Community Features to collaborate and communicate with other LinkedIn users. These include Groups, Answers, and Company Pages. Groups keep you informed and in touch with other LinkedIn users of the same interests and passion. You can either join an existing one already or create your own! The best way to expand your social (and business) circles is to add great value to discussions when you participate. Keep in mind, you are still communicating as a business and the persona you created for that. In discussions, you will, of course, want to appear personable and friendly- but on a platform like LinkedIn, there is room for greater formality and professionalism than you might present on alternative networks such as Twitter or Facebook.

Answers is an excellent way to connect with similar-minded colleagues as well as share your expertise with others, promoting your profile – and business – indirectly. You can connect by asking pressing and intelligent questions and let other experts chip in their $100's worth of advice and in the process, connect with them. You can also toot your own horn (not too obvious, though) by answering questions as an expert too. Both methods are a valuable way to form additional connections and to show off your intellect and thoughtfulness, provided you do so in a humble, honest way. Both asking and answering eloquently worded and reasonable questions can earn you the respect of other businesses and individuals you will encounter on LinkedIn.

Lastly, you can use LinkedIn's Company Pages to look for business partner companies as well as spy on competing ones. This can help you determine the most effective marketing strategies to use, as it allows you to consider markets your competitors have not yet tapped. It also enables you to take inspiration from their current or previous campaigns, modifying them to make them your own, of course, or explore new territories that they are lacking in. Further, you can set up a page for your own business where you can show your expertise in your industry or niche and indirectly promote your company or business. Here, you can publish key information about your business such as website address, business address, and company or business description. Be sure to be thorough and accurate in your descriptions.

CHAPTER 11
PINTEREST MARKETING

Pinterest, like Instagram, specializes in pictures and images. As such, in order to use it successfully, you must master creatively putting your products and services into image form in a manner that catches the eye and entices your potential customers. Pinterest enables users to pin images that appeal to them to their Pinterest page. Each pin includes a link to an external site, such as that of your business. Pinterest works similarly to a search engine, where users can search for keywords or phrases to find applicable images that suit their fancy.

You might wonder whether you should choose Pinterest or Instagram considering the similarities. Pinterest can work very well at boosting your SEO sources and has such should be considered as an alternative or addition to Instagram. It will also depend on, of course, on the demographic you are looking to target. Both platforms boast high numbers of women, but Instagram features more teenagers while Pinterest usually markets itself to those with crafty or other creative interests and pursuits. Those using Instagram usually are seeking personal experiences and unusual pictures, whereas on Pinterest individuals are seeking tips, tutorials, and inspiration, primarily. You can certainly utilize both resources, but tailor your content accordingly, or select the one that suits your product.

Pinterest enables you to create beautiful and spectacular themed boards, which are collections of pictures that can tell a story or pull at the heartstrings if assembled and ordered carefully. You can utilize this feature to represent a product or a promotion and to encourage people to pin images from your Pinterest board, raising further awareness of your business. You can pin images, articles, tips- anything informative, thought-provoking, helpful, or otherwise compelling will do, though be sure to select something that compliments the goals of your business as well as inspiring your customers. As always, use hashtags appropriately in order to generate greater interest in your company's social media accounts.

Pinterest also enables you to gain the support and recognition of your customers and future customers as well as that of other businesses that you might want to work with by way of pinning content they post. Doing so links back to their page, and they might, in turn, support you as well, which can generate a substantial amount of increased traffic to your website. If you put together creative, useful, and visually appealing Pinterest boards, it can be a great resource in getting more visits to your site, which can be particularly useful if you are just starting out and still trying to generate awareness. Instagram falls somewhat short here as very little will be linked back to your other sites and that can make it more challenging if you are still in the early stages of conjuring up customers at all.

Be warned, though- Pinterest will not show those interested in your pins everything you post. The platform recommends content for its users based on their interests, which it generates from things they've viewed and pinned over a period of time. As such, if your own contributions are not entirely consistent some of what you share might never be viewed by your prospective customers at all. If you are still unsure between Pinterest and Instagram, considering using LinkedIn to scrutinize the choices of your competitors. If they all seem to favor one over the other, it may very well suit your products and services better. That said, a pioneering attitude is not without it's merits and if you embrace the less popular choice you might find an opportunity to shine.

With about 70 million users and unique opportunities to share curated content and generate vastly increased views of your other sites, Pinterest is a social media platform well worth considering, particularly if you are targeting young adult women as part of your intended demographic.

CHAPTER 12
GOOGLE+ MARKETING

Google+ focuses on joining and creating communities, wherein you can share links, blog posts, and other content promoting your business, as well as allowing you to view and discuss the content shared by others. Like with most social media platforms, it is very important to engage with and communicate with your future customers. Throwing a bunch of links promoting your business at them will feel too impersonal. But once you gain their trust, it can make for a comfortable place in which to interact with customers and share business links, promotions, and thoughtful or interesting posts. Naturally, depending on the nature of the community or communities you start or join, you will want to customize your posts and contributions to suit your audience. You would do well to join a number of communities to maximize your success with Google+. After all, even within your target market, you will encounter diverse people with varying interests- learning what they are likely to enjoy and become a contributing member of those communities will enable you to gain the most conversions. You can reuse the same link in each community, provided it is fitting, but make sure you customize your comments to the community so that your links and content make sense and are appropriately personalized.

Google+ really shines with it comes to SEO. Getting comments, shares, and plus ones on your contributions on Google+ works wonders when it comes to getting your website ranked highly in search engines, not least among them Google itself. Due to the obvious affiliation of Google and Google+, Google creates a back-link to articles, websites, and other content you contribute to, generating additional SEO hits for your company. Over time, you can even gain an Authority rank, which comes from having a large community circle with lots of activity, both yours and others in reference to you. In essence, it enables you to gain a higher ranking due to having a superior online reputation, and in doing so grants you an increased rating when determining who ranks highest in search engine optimization results. This is not an easy rank to come by, of course, but investing time into Google+ to accomplish it can reap significant results for your business.

Another important thing to note about Google+ is that through Google Hangouts, it is linked to Youtube, enabling you to pair perfectly using Google+ and Youtube seamlessly. This increases your search engine results across both platforms, particularly if you are ever inclined to include some live video streams, which have a number of benefits. They rank higher in search engine optimization results than traditional methods of filming the video prior to posting. They also truly demonstrate your charisma and competence to your customers, as well as increase their trust and respect for you since it is much, much harder to fake or hide things while live screening a video.

Be warned that Google will track your activity. This can be a blessing or a curse depending on what you make of it, but if you use it will, it can be a fantastic platform to select due to it's Youtube collaboration and it's propensity to rank you highly in search engine optimization results.

CHAPTER 13
TUMBLR MARKETING

Tumblr is another primarily visual social media networking with an ever-increasing amount of young users serving as its primary audience. You can include written works and articles on Tumblr, but its ideal use is best suited to pictures, animated GIFs, and videos, short films, or movies. Audio files are also getting increased attention on Tumblr and therefore might be a good area to potentially explore if your business lends itself to such.

On Tumblr, a sound strategy to gain followers and attention is simply to follow others, preferably those within your target market. Tumblr does not display the number of people you are following, or, for that matter, the number of people who follow you. This enables you to safely get to know your audience and customize your own posts and content to suit their interests. It is even a platform that enables you to post, follow, or otherwise appreciate fan created content based on your products, services, or business- a flattering gesture demonstrating loyalty and spreading awareness for your company. In this way, you can engage customers by getting them directly involved and effectively enable them to do some of your advertising for you. If you run contests for your followers to generate fan created content for you and offer a prize for the best creation, you will have an excellent promotion that is fun for everyone involved. I highly suggest letting the community vote on the best one in such competitions, making it an exciting experience even for those who do not directly participate. Any submissions can be used and appreciated in your own marketing campaigns, both on Tumblr and on other social media sites.

Like with Pinterest and Instagram, making things visually striking will really appeal to the Tumblr community. Unlike those two choices, however, hashtags are not an option on Tumblr, so you have to include compelling keywords to get your posts and content noticed. Aim to feature eye-catching pieces that trigger an emotional response, or something humorous, and you are likely to go far on Tumblr.

CHAPTER 14

OTHER METHODS OF SOCIAL MEDIA MARKETING

In addition to the many resources and strategies proposed above there are other forms of social media marketing and advertising that you might consider trying when growing your business. We'll take the time to discuss a few of these options in this section.

We will begin our discussion with Yelp. Yelp allows businesses to create profiles for themselves, which they can display and share to the community. These commonly include location, products and services offered, pictures or other images, and methods of contacting them. Additionally, a company can link it's website from it's Yelp profile, enabling customers to easily click the link and generating more traffic on your website. The goal of Yelp is primarily for customers to review and rate your business on a scale going from one through five. They can praise or criticize features they did or did not like publicly as part of their review. Additionally, companies being reviewed as well as other individuals can respond to their reviews in order to enable the two-way communication so essential of social media. If you gain positive reviews on Yelp, it will surely raise the reputation of your business and increase your customer base and sales, so it is worth taking a bit of time to set up a representative and professional profile for your company there.

An additional social media platform that has existed for quite a long time now is simply blogging. While they no longer enjoy the same popularity as they once did, considering the wide availability and subsequent popularity of newer and fresher social media options these days, they can still be a useful tool to take advantage of. Blogs allow you the opportunity to express more via writing about your business or products. You can easily have a blog as part of your website that you can update with any new and exciting products or services you offer as well as other interesting business developments. You can use your other social media accounts to link to your blog when it is fitting, and it can be a fun place to do promotions such as giveaways. Additionally, you can follow and comment on the blogs of others, and in some cases people might review your products and/or services on their own personal blogs. If their reviews are positive, it can certainly increase your prestige and your customer base, as anyone following their blog will suddenly view you in a favorable light.

Finally, you should consider the option of social commerce, which is closely linked to many other social media platforms and in many cases, can be utilized simultaneously. It usually involves aiding customers in getting advice on what they might like, and then instructions on how to find and purchase the items and services they require or desire. Like most other forms of social media, it requires trust and communication. Parts of social commerce include user reviews and ratings, as is featured on Yelp, as well as recommendations, apps, and shopping communities that discuss this interest and share likes and favorites with one another. Tools such as quizzes or polls that direct consumers to products that they might like are frequent components in the social commerce world, as are applications that allow your customers to share their shopping experiences with their entire social network at the press of a button. Social commerce is, primarily, about building and cultivating a reputation. Having unusual or limited edition items and specialized shopping services will make potential customers want to seize the opportunity to make a purchase while they still can- and then they will share it with others, effectively advertising for your company. In doing so more traffic is brought in and the cycle continues. Extremely popular sites that utilize social commerce fully include, but are not limited to, Etsy, Groupon, Cafepress, and even Pinterest. Notably, social commerce is an ever increasing market, and there are some experts who predict that 2016 will be a very successful year for social commerce, so now might be the right time to get your business involved in it.

CHAPTER 15

UP AND COMING OPTIONS: SOMETHING TO CONSIDER

In addition to all the great options listed above, I'd like to take a few moments to look into new and exciting options at the forefront of social media. The social media platforms we discussed in greater depth earlier are all juggernauts in their field, and most of them have been around and holding strong for quite some time now. Consistency on such things is valuable and a good way to ensure you sign up with a strong and proven outlet for your marketing needs, and as such those options should never be understated.

That said, they are not the only options out there. With each passing year, technology and current trends fluctuate and evolve. New and emerging social media platforms begin to burst forth into bloom. Certainly there are greater risks with selecting a newer and less popular platform, but a pioneering spirit is sometimes the key to success. If you have a more adventurous soul than most and are not one to back down over a little risk, you may want to consider some of the options that we will discuss in this chapter. Small risks sometimes result in major rewards, and these are areas you may very well outpace and overtake your competitors in by being an early adopter and user of alternative social media choices. If you don't find something that fully satisfies you in our original list, or if you want to explore uncharted territory, be on the lookout for up and coming options: they've got what you need.

CONCLUSION
COMING TOGETHER

Technology is changing our lives in so many different ways that only a generation ago were figments of the imagination. Of course, the single biggest change is the Internet, which has pretty much leveled the playing field – in terms of marketing - and has also made business more competitive than ever.

As you learned in this book, social media marketing is an indirect way of selling – compared to traditional marketing – and primarily engages prospects and customers using high quality and unique content, which makes them feel increasingly more connected to products and services. Particularly with Facebook, social media marketing can help you reach more of your intended market at significantly less cost than traditional marketing. Talk about the most bang for your marketing bucks!

To be done successfully, we learned that social media marketing has to target your customers as individuals and make them feel valued and engaged. It involves more creative and entertaining ideas than traditional marketing in order to ensure potential clients will enjoy it and desire more of what your business has to offer. It also involves a more personal touch and therefore greater degrees of friendliness and sociability. It is the goal of every business utilizing social media that presenting itself in such ways will encourage customers to trust it and to eventually become loyal.

You can't afford to brush aside social media marketing because this is the way of the future. In fact, the future is already here! Not to discount traditional marketing as totally useless or irrelevant but social media marketing can significantly help you market your products even better, especially if used to complement traditional marketing activities. Failure to do so at this point in time can increase your business' risk for decreased or stagnant sales or worse, failure. Even if you think it's a temporary, spur of the moment sort of fad, it is still well worth utilizing. The benefits and rewards have endless potential, and the time and money you have to invest is low. Times have changed, and this is a part of the reality we live in now. Part of running and marketing a successful business is adaptability, and social media networking and advertising is definitely a part of the world we live in. Any business aiming to be successful should strive to adapt to this new marketing trend.

If you'd like to get more in-depth tips and tactics for mastering social media marketing and skyrocketing your start-up, check out the book *500 Social Media Marketing Tips: Essential Advice, Hints, And Strategy For Business: Facebook, Twitter, Pinterest, Google+, Youtube, Instagram, Linkedin, And More!* by Andrew Macarthy, which is another excellent resource on mastering social media marketing. Now that you've read this book, you're in a very good position to understand the tips and tricks presented by Andrew Macarthy in this paperback book.

Here's to your social media marketing success!

If you received value from this book, then I would like to ask you for a favor. Would you be kind enough to leave a review for this book on Amazon?

Thank you so much!

Cheers!